Present Perfect Continuous

Italian does not have a present perfect continuous tense:

I have been studying Italian for six years (and still study it).

To express an action that began in the past, continues into the present and is still being done, Italian uses the following construction:

present tense + **da** + period of time

Here is an example:

Studio l'italiano **da** otto anni.

I have been studying Italian for eight years.

The

The preposition (**la preposizione**) **da** has some important uses that should be memorized since they are commonly heard and used in everyday conversations and are necessary for passive constructions.

Here are some of the most common uses for the preposition:

✦ place

As if Italian was not confusing enough already with its prepositions for going to places, the preposition **da** provides an extra level of complication. Use *this* preposition when you are going to a friend or family member's home, the mechanic, the doctor's office and a few other places:

dall'avvocato	*to the lawyer's office*
dal dentista	*to the dentist/dentist's office*
da Maria	*to Maria's (house)*
da me/te/lui/lei	*at my/your/his/her house*
da noi/voi/loro	*at our/your/their house*
dal meccanico	*to the mechanic's*
dal medico	*to the doctor/doctor's office*
dallo zio	*at my uncle's (house)*

✦ time

The preposition **da** can also be used to mark important periods in one's life:

Da bambino credevo a Babbo Natale!

As a child I used to believe in Santa Claus!

More Time with *da*

In Italian, **da** is often used with the preposition **a** to indicate the duration of an action. The preposition **da** (*from*) tells us the starting point, while the preposition **a** (*to*) indicates the end:

Non credo di volere andare a teatro! Quell'opera teatrale è in programma **dalle** 19 **alle** 23 e devo svegliarmi presto domattina.

I don't believe I want to go to the theater. That play is scheduled to go from 7 PM to 11 PM, and I have to get up early tomorrow morning.

⁺ origin

Just as we saw with the preposition **di**, the preposition **da** can also be used to convey origin *but with the verb* **venire**:

Siamo americani. Veniamo **da** St. Paul! La conosci?

We are American. We come from St. Paul! Do you know it?

⁺ movement

The preposition **da** is also used to indicate movement *from* a place:

Guardiamo bene la mappa o ci perdiamo: noi siamo qui. **Da** qui, dobbiamo prendere questa strada per arrivare al porto.

Let's have a good look at the map or we'll get lost: we are here. From here, we have to take this street to get to the port.

⁺ agent

Da is used in passive constructions to mean *by*:

La palla è stata lanciata **da** Marcello.

The ball was thrown by Marcello.

This page intentionally left blank -- use it to take notes as you study!

This page intentionally left blank -- use it to take notes as you study!

Piccole Guide: Volume 1

PREPOSIZIONI

A short guide on the correct use of Italian prepositions

by Daniele Laudadio & Keith Preble

Acknowledgements:
Special thanks to Mary D., Angela L., and Nick N. for taking the time to proofread the language guide before its publication. Your feedback, advice, and corrections were much appreciated!

I would also like to thank all of the followers of Parola del Giorno (www.paroladelgiorno.com) for your years of support. Grazie mille!

Lastly, a *very* special thank you to all my friends in Italy for helping me develop and grow my language skills over the last 15+ years!

Exercise Supplement:
Volume 1 of *Piccole Guide* comes with a free exercise supplement that can be downloaded at your convenience from our web site. This is an additional pdf document that contains exercises to help you practice what you have learned in this short guide.

Visit our web site at the address below to learn how you can get your free exercise supplement:

http://paroladelgiorno.com/piccole-guide-little-guides/

If you have any questions, please contact us at info@paroladelgiorno.com.

PREPOSIZIONI

A short guide on the correct use of Italian prepositions

Simple Prepositions

Simple prepositions are single words that act only as prepositions: **di**, **a**, **da**, **in**, **con**, **su**, **per**, **fra/tra**.

Articulated Prepositions

Simple prepositions (only **a**, **con**, **da**, **di**, **in**, and **su**) change form and combine with the definite article to form **articulated prepositions**.

Improper Prepositions

These are prepositions that can also be other parts of speech, such as verbs, adjectives, and adverbs: **durante**, **insieme**, and **senza**.

Phrasal Prepositions

These prepositions are two or more words where the final word in the phrase is a simple preposition: **per mezzo di**, **a causa di**, etc.

Introduction

Using prepositions in Italian can be maddening at times! They do not always equate to what one is familiar with in English, so it often requires a lot of flexible thinking.

This guide contains four sections and will explore the four types of prepositions: **simple**, **articulated**, **improper** and **phrasal** prepositions.

How to use this guide

We hope that this short guide will serve as a quick reference guide to students who are learning Italian. There are many other books on the market that go into greater depth on preposition usage. However, for most students, this short guide should serve to be an excellent resource for mastering the common uses of Italian prepositions.

Important points of grammar, vocabulary notes and other important information will appear in the left-hand margins throughout the guide to help facilitate learning and help with understanding key differences between the two languages.

Appendices

The end of our short language guide features some useful appendices that contain important lists of verbs, adjectives, or nouns with their respective prepositions.

1

Section 1: Simple Prepositions

Section 1 will explore the seven simple prepositions, their common uses and some important points of grammar.

Italian has the following simple prepositions:

- di
- a
- da
- in
- con
- su
- per
- tra/fra

Almost all of the simple prepositions can be combined with the definite article, <u>but</u> **per** and **fra/tra** are *never* articulated.

The preposition: *di*

The preposition (**la preposizione**) **di** has a variety of uses in Italian. It should be noted that prepositions do not always translate easily from Italian to English, and there can be many meanings depending on how the preposition is used.

Here are some of the most common uses of **di**:

✦ possession

In Italian, the preposition **di** is used to convey possession. Whereas English often uses an apostrophe + *s* to convey possession (Marco's jacket), Italian uses **di** + *possessor*:

Questa è l'auto **di** mia sorella. Stai attento a non sporcarla, lei è una maniaca della pulizia!

This is my sister's car. Pay attention not to get it dirty, she is a neat freak!

✦ authorship

Use the preposition **di** to say that a book, article, poem, etc. is written by a particular person:

Il vecchio e il mare è un libro importante **di** Ernest Hemingway.

The Old Man and the Sea is an important book by Ernest Hemingway.

✦ material

To say that something is made of a certain material, Italian uses the preposition **di**:

Voglio comprare una borsa nuova ma non so se prenderla **di** cuoio o **di** stoffa. Quale materiale mi consigli?

Comparisons

One of the uses of the preposition **di** is with comparisons with the adverbs **più** and **meno**, expressing *than*:

Marco è più carino **di** Giorgio.

Marco is cuter than Giorgio.

Giovanna è meno fortunata **di** noi.

Giovanna is less fortunate than us.

Comparisons can also be formed with the preposition **a** when comparing two people or things that are similar:

I mio nuovo smartphone ha molte più funzioni **rispetto a** quello che avevo prima.

My new smartphone has many more functions than what I had before.

Whereas **da** is used to compare two people or things that are dissimilar:

Questa sciarpa è completamente **diversa da** quella che ti avevo detto di comprarmi. Mi ascolti quando parlo?

This shoe is completely different from what I had told you to buy me. Do you listen to me when I speak?

I want to buy a new bag, but I don't know whether to get it in leather or cloth. Which material would you suggest?

⁺ **comparisons**

The preposition **di** is used (along with **che**) in making comparisons, translating as *than* (see sidebar for more information on **comparisons**).

Clara mi ha detto che il tuo regalo le è piaciuto più **di** tutti gli altri.

Clara told me she liked your gift more than all the others.

⁺ **time expressions**

The preposition **di** is used in a variety of time expressions in Italian:

di mattina	*in the morning*
di notte	*at night*
d'inverno	*in the winter*
del pomeriggio	*in the afternoon*
d'estate	*in the summer*

⁺ **origins**

When you are asked where you are from in Italian, the preposition **di** is often heard. Your response with the verb **essere** also requires the preposition:

Di dove sei?

Where are you from?

Sono **del** Michigan.

I'm from Michigan.

✦ partitive

To indicate indefinite quantities, the preposition **di** is used in its articulated form to convey *some*:

Se più tardi vai dal fruttivendolo, mi compreresti **delle** mele, **delle** fragole e **dei** kiwi? Stasera voglio fare una crostata di frutta.

If you go to the fruit stand later, would you buy me some apples, strawberries and some kiwi? Tonight I want to make a fruit crostata.

Complemento di termine *or* Indirect Object

In Italian, the preposition **a** always precedes the indirect object (**il complemento di termine**) when the indirect object is a noun or proper noun:

Ho detto **a quello scemo** che non andiamo alla festa di Cinzia prima delle 22. Perché Marco continua a chiedere **a Maria e Tiziana** quando ci andiamo?

I told that idiot we are not going to Cinzia's party until 10:00 PM. Why does Marco continue to ask Maria and Tiziana when we are going?

It is important to note that some verbs that take direct objects in English take indirect objects in Italian. Here's a brief list:

- chiedere
- dire
- sembrare
- telefonare

The preposition: a

The preposition (**la preposizione**) **a** has a variety of uses in Italian:

Here are some of the most common uses of **a**:

✦ geography

When going/coming/being in a particular city or place, the preposition **a** is used:

Questo weekend girerò tutta l'Italia: ieri ero **a** Milano, oggi sto andando **a** Roma e domani sarò **a** Palermo.

This weekend I will tour all of Italy: yesterday I was in Milan, today I am going to Rome, and tomorrow I will be in Palermo.

The following places typically require the preposition **a**:

all'aeroporto	*at the airport*
al bar	*at the bar*
a casa	*at home*
al cinema	*to the movies*
all'estero	*overseas; abroad*
a letto	*to bed*
al mare	*to the beach/seaside*
a scuola	*at school*
alla stazione	*at the station*
a teatro	*to the theater*

✦ **distance**

Many students of Italian are often not taught or forget this rule. It is important to remember that the preposition **a** must precede a distance needed to get from one place to another:

Piazza del Popolo si trova **a** dieci minuti a piedi da qui. Non è lontana.

The Piazza del Popolo is a ten minute walk from here. It isn't far.

✦ **time**

Use the preposition **a** to express a time that some event is going to take place:

Maria, dove sono le chiavi? Il mio colloquio inizia **alle 14** e non posso essere in ritardo!

Maria, where are the keys? My interview starts at 2:00 PM, and I cannot be late!

Rooms of the house

The preposition **in** is used with rooms of the house - these expressions *do not* use the articulated preposition (unless the room of the house is modified):

in bagno   *in the bathroom*

in camera   *in the room*

in cucina   *in the kitchen*

in giardino   *in the garden*

in sala   *in the room*

in salotto   *in the living room*

If the room is modified by an adjective or prepositional phrase, the preposition is articulated:

nella cucina <u>di Antonia</u>

The preposition: in

The preposition (**la preposizione**) **in** is used not only for places but also with time expressions and to convey the various modes of transportation.

Here are some of the most common uses:

✦ **modes of transport**

The preposition **in** is used with modes of transport:

in aereo	*by plane*
in autobus	*by bus*
in bici(cletta)	*by bike*
in macchina	*by car*
in metro(politana)	*by metro/underground/subway*
in moto(cicletta)	*by motorcycle*
in nave	*by boat*
in treno	*by train*

There are two exceptions:

a piedi	*on foot*
a cavallo	*on horseback*

✦ **time**

The preposition **in** is used with time expressions to convey how much time it took for an action to be completed:

Grazie a Dio la metro funzionava senza problemi! Sono arrivato **in** dieci minuti per quel colloquio importante.

Thank God the metro was working without any problems! I got to that important interview in 10 minutes.

<u>Do not</u> use the preposition **in** to convey how much time must pass *before* an action takes place! Use **tra/ fra**:

Fra un'ora devo uscire: il colloquio comincia alle 11 ma con la metro è sempre meglio partire un po' presto, no?

In an hour I have to go out: the interview starts at 11, but with the metro it is always better to leave a bit early, no?

✦ places

Just like the prepositions **a** and **da**, the preposition **in** is used to indicate *being/going to* a place. Generally, places that end in -ia take the preposition **in**:

in farmacia	*at/in the pharmacy*
in libreria	*at/in the bookstore*
in pizzeria	*at/in the pizzeria*
in trattoria	*at/in the trattoria*

In is also used with a variety of places:

in banca	*at/in the bank*
in negozio	*at/in the store*
in ospedale	*at/in the hospital*
in ufficio	*at/in the office*

The preposition **in** is also used in a variety of other expressions:

in campagna	*in the country(side)*
in centro	*downtown*
in città	*in town*
in montagna	*in the mountains*
in vacanza	*on vacation/on holidays*

From start to finish with *tra* & *fra*

Just like the prepositions **da** and **a** are used to express how long an action lasts, the prepositions **tra/fra** can also be used:

Non so a che ora comincia la riunione. Il capo ha detto **fra** le 14 e le 15. Secondo me sarebbe meglio che si arrivasse alle 14 per evitare problemi.

I don't know what time the meeting starts. The boss said between 2:00 PM and 3:00 PM. In my opinion it would be better to arrive at 2:00 PM to avoid any problems.

In this example, the meeting could start at anytime between 2:00 PM and 3:00 PM.

However, **tra/fra** can also be used to indicate when an action will take place in a certain period of time:

Marco andrà in Polonia **fra** il 6 and il 21 giungo.

Marco will go to Poland from the 6th to the 21st of June.

✦ **geography**

The preposition **in** is used to convey *to* a country or other geographic locality that is not a city:

Quest'estate io e mia moglie vogliamo andare **in** Danimarca.

This summer my wife and I want to go to Denmark.

Ti va di fare una passeggiata **in** spiaggia più tardi?

Do you feel like taking a walk on the beach later?

A Milano c'è molto smog, per respirare aria buona ti devi spostare **in** montagna.

There is a lot of smog in Milan, and in order to breathe good air, you have to head to the mountains.

The preposition: con

The preposition (**la preposizione**) **con** generally means *with* in English:

✦ togetherness

The preposition **con** is used to indicate *togetherness* as well as how something is:

Vivo ancora **con** i miei genitori.

I am still living with my parents.

✦ getting married

The Italian verb **sposarsi** - to get married - uses the preposition **con** (*to*):

Marco si sposa **con** Antonietta questa domenica.

Marco is getting married to Antonietta this Sunday.

su di + *tonic pronoun*

Improper prepositions are not the only preposition to require a simple preposition at times.

The preposition **su** requires the preposition **di** before tonic pronouns:

Carlo ha scritto un'email **su di me**. Non mi piace quello che ha scritto.

Carlo wrote an email about me. I do not like what he wrote.

The preposition: su

The preposition (**la preposizione**) **su** generally means *on* or *about*:

⁺ topics of discussion

The preposition **su** is used to indicate *about*, such as what people are talking about, reading about, etc:

Scusami un attimo, Marina, ma sto leggendo un articolo **sulla** politica italiana e il voto di fiducia.

Excuse me a moment, Marina, but I am reading an article on Italian politics and the confidence vote.

Mio padre dice che i documentari **sulla Sicilia** sono sempre pieni di luoghi comuni! **Sull'isola** c'è molto di più della mafia e della criminalità.

My father says documentaries on Sicily are always full of cliches! On the island there is much more than the mafia and criminality!

⁺ location

The preposition **su** can also indicate where an object is or lies:

Il portafoglio? Certo che l'ho visto! Si trova **sulla** scrivania.

The wallet? Of course I saw it! It is on the desk.

Gianna, non mettere il latte **sullo** scaffale dell'armadietto! Sai che preferisco il latte freddo! Mettilo dentro il frigo.

Gianna, don't put the milk on the cabinet shelf. You know I prefer cold milk! Put it in the fridge.

✦ ratios & proportions

Often when reading newspapers, the preposition **su** is used to convey certain general statistics, such as *1 out of 5 people*, etc:

Due italiani **su** tre preferiscono passare le vacanze al mare. Si vede che le spiagge sono molto popolari in Italia!

Two Italians out of three prefer to spend their vacation at the beach. You can see that beaches are very popular in Italy!

The preposition: per

The preposition (**la preposizione**) **per** generally means *for* but also has a few other meanings and uses:

✦ **per** + *infinitve*

The preposition **per** can be used with infinitives to convey *in order to*:

Devo andare alla posta **per** inviare un pacco importante.

I have to go to the post office to send an important package.

✦ **stare per** + *infinitive*

Per, when used with the verb **stare**, means *to be about to* do something:

Mamma, che fai in cucina? L'acqua bolle: stai **per** cucinare qualcosa?

Mamma, what are you doing in the kitchen? The water is boiling: are you about to cook something?

✦ **passare per** = *to pass by*

The verb **passare** is often used with the preposition **per** to convey *passing by* a certain place:

Marco, hai visto il cane? È passato **per** il salotto?

Marco, did you see the dog? Did he pass by the living room?

✦ **destination**

The preposition **per** can be used to convey *to* or *for* a certain destination when used with the verb **partire**:

Scusi, signore, lei sa se questo treno parte per Milano?

Excuse me, sir, do you know if this train is going to Milan?

+ time

Per is used to say how long an action continues to occur or had occured:

Ieri la metro non funzionava e ho dovuto camminare **per** due ore. Pensavo che ci fosse lo sciopero...

Yesterday, the metro was down, and I had to walk for two hours. I thought there was a strike...

From start to finish with *tra* & *fra*

Just like the prepositions **da** and **a** are used to express how long an action lasts, the prepositions **tra/fra** can also be used:

Non so a che ora comincia la riunione. Il capo ha detto **fra** le 14 e le 15. Secondo me sarebbe meglio che si arrivasse alle 14 per evitare problemi.

I don't know what time the meeting starts. The boss said between 2:00 PM and 3:00 PM. In my opinion it would be better to arrive at 2:00 PM to avoid any problems.

In this example, the meeting could start at anytime between 2:00 PM and 3:00 PM.

However, **tra/fra** can also be used to indicate when an action will take place in a certain period of time:

Marco andrà in Polonia **fra** il 6 and il 21 giungo.

Marco will go to Poland from the 6th to the 21st of June.

The prepositions: tra & fra

The prepositions (**le preposizioni**) **tra** and **fra** can generally be used interchangeably - there is no difference in their meaning. The choice of one or the other is usually a personal preference, but Italians tend to avoid alliterations with these two prepositions.

Let's look at their use below:

+ between

Tra and **fra** can be used indicate where something is and to mean *between*:

Secondo te, è meglio che noi mettiamo il divano **tra** le <u>fi</u>nestre o più vicino alla scrivania?

In your opinion it is better that we put the sofa between the windows or closer to the desk?

+ among

Tra and **fra** can be used to mean *among*:

Alla manifestazione Francesco ci ha avvisato che c'erano poliziotti **tra** i manifestanti.

At the protest Francesco informed us there were police officers among the protesters.

+ time

Tra and **fra** can be used indicate how much time *must first pass* before an action will take place:

Marco arriverà **fra** un'ora, giusto in tempo per la partita. Non ti preoccupare: è sempre in orario.

Marco will arrive in an hour, just in time for the match. Don't worry: he is always punctual.

Section 2: Articulated prepositions

Section 2 will explore *articulated prepositions* (**preposizioni articolate**), which combine with the *definite article* (**l'articolo determinativo**).

The prepositions **a**, **di**, **da**, **su**, **in** and **con**.

The prepositions **tra/fra** and **per** are never articulated.

Articulated Prepositions

Articulated preposition can be seen in the table below.

Note that the preposition **con** can be articulated or not depending on the situation or context. The preposition **con** is not articulated with the definite article **l'**.

As a rule, the definite article and the preposition typically are always combined, although there are exceptions, which we will explore on the next page.

Be sure when writing and speaking that you choose the correct articulated preposition. It might help to remember that the articulated preposition must match the gender and number of the noun that follows it.

	il	l'	lo	i	gli	la	le
a	al	all'	allo	ai	agli	alla	alle
di	del	dell'	dello	dei	degli	dalla	dalle
da	dal	dall'	dallo	dai	dagli	dalla	dalle
in	nel	nell'	nello	nei	negli	nella	nelle
su	sul	sull'	sullo	sui	sugli	sulla	sulle
con	col / con il	con l'	collo / con lo	coi / con i	cogli / con gli	colla / con la	colle / con le

Rules regarding articulated prepositions

As a general rule, you should always combine the preposition with the definite article. There are some exceptions:

1. Remember that with members of the family, the possessive adjective is used without the definite article:

Mia madre va al cinema. Non mi va di accompagnarla.

My mother is going to the cinema. I don't feel like going with her.

Perché? Non passi mai tempo con **tua madre**.

Why? You never spend time with your mother.

2. The definite article is not used with rooms of the house:

Marco, va' **in cucina** e prendimi qualcosa da bere!

Marco, go to the kitchen and get me something to drink!

Section 3: Improper prepositions

Section 3 identifies some common improper prepositions (**preposizioni improprie**).

What are improper prepositions?

Improper prepositions (**preposizioni improprie**) are prepositions that also function as another part of speech.

In Italian, improper prepositions can be nouns, adjectives, adverbs, or verbs.

They are sometimes combined with simple prepositions, too.

Below is a list of the most common improper prepositions you will encounter in Italian:

attraverso	*across*
circa	*around, about*
contro	*against*
davanti (a)	*in front of*
dentro (a)	*inside, inside of*
dopo	*after*
dietro	*behind*
eccetto	*except*
entro	*within*
fuori	*outside*
insieme (a)	*together*
intorno (a)	*around*
lontano (da)	*far (from)*
lungo	*along*
nonostante	*despite, in spite of*
prima	*before*

presso	*at, near*
secondo	*according to;*
	in my/your/his/their opinion
senza (di)	*without*
sotto	*under*
sopra (di)	*above*
tramite	*by, through*
tranne	*except*
vicino (a)	*near*

Section 4: Phrasal Prepositions

Section 4 identifies some common phrasal prepositions (**locuzioni prepositive**).

What are phrasal prepositions?

Phrasal prepositions are constructions that are made up of two simple prepositions and another part of speech, such as **a causa di**.

Common phrasal prepositions

Here is a list of some of the more common phrasal prepositions that you are bound to encounter as you learn Italian:

a causa di	*because of; due to*
a fianco di	*beside; next to*
al di là di	*beyond*
al di qua di	*on this side of*
al largo di	*off*
allo scopo di	*for*
a titolo di	*by way of*
di fronte a	*in front of; opposite; facing*
in base a	*under*
in cima a	*atop; on top of*
in compagnia di	*with; in someone's company*
in mezzo a	*between; among*
in quanto a	*concerning; regarding; as for*
in virtù di	*by virtue of; in accordance with*
per opera di	*by means of; due to*
per mezzo di	*by; through*

Appendix 1

The verbs in Appendix 1 require the preposition **a** before an infinitive.

Learning Tip: There is no easy way to learn these verb/preposition combinations. We suggest purchasing some index cards and a marker/pen, and writing the Italian verb and preposition on one side and the English equivalent on the other!

Grammar Note: Note that some of these verbs also require direct or indirect objects to complete their meaning (for example, the verb **insegnare**).

Maria is the indirect object. In Italian, it is:

insegnare a qualcuno a fare qualcosa

abituarsi + a	*to be used to [doing something]*
andare + a	*to go to [do something]*
cominciare + a	*to start to [do something]*
continuare + a	*to continue to [do something]*
divertirsi + a	*to enjoy [doing something]*
farcela + a	*to manage to [do something]*
imparare + a	*to learn to [do something]*
iniziare + a	*to start to [do something]*
insegnare + a	*to teach to [do something]*

Marco **ha insegnato** <u>a Maria</u>* **a** pescare quando siamo andati al lago l'anno scorso.

Marco taught <u>Maria</u> to fish when we went to the lake last year.

insistere + a	*to insist on [doing something]*

Perchè **insisti a litigare** con tua madre? Ha sempre ragione!

Why do you insist on arguing with your mother? She is always right!

mettersi + a	*to start to [do something]*
passare + a	*to go by/to pass by [to do something]*
provare + a	*to try [to do something]*
restare + a	*to stay [to do something]*
rinunciare + a	*to give up [doing something]*
riuscire + a	*to manage to, to succeed in [do/doing something]*
soffrire + a	*to be unable to, to not bear [doing something]*

Appendix 2

The verbs in Appendix 2 require the preposition **di** before an infinitive.

Learning Tip: There is no easy way to learn these verb/ preposition combinations. We suggest purchasing some index cards and a marker/pen, and writing the Italian verb and preposition on one side and the English equivalent on the other!

cercare + di	*to try to [do something]*
credere + di*	*to believe, to think*

Credo di essere lo studente più bravo a scuola.

I think I'm the most capable student at school.

I believe to be the most capable student at school.

dimenticarsi + di	*to forget to [do something]*
dimenticare + di	
finire + di	*to finish [doing something]*
ricordarsi + di	*to remember to [do something]*
scegliere + di	*to choose to [do something]*
smettere + di	*to stop [doing something]*
sperare + di	*to hope to [do something]*
sognare + di	*to dream of [doing something]*

Mario e Giovanna sognano di andare negli Stati Uniti! Vogliono visitare Hollywood perché amano il cinema americano.

Mario and Giovanna dream of going to the U.S. They want to visit Hollywood because they love American films.

tentare + di	*to attempt [to do something]*

*Verbs only take the subjunctive when there is a change of subject. In this example, the subject remains the same (**io**). Instead of **che** and the subjunctive, use the preposition **di** + **infinitive**.

Appendix 3

The verbs in Appendix 3 require the preposition **di** before an infinitive; they also require an indirect object, too.

Learning Tip: There is no easy way to learn these verb/preposition combinations. We suggest purchasing some index cards and a marker/pen, and writing the Italian verb and preposition on one side and the English equivalent on the other!

chiedere (a qualcuno) + di   *to ask (someone to do something)*

concedere (a qualcuno) + di   *to allow (someone to do something)*

dire (a qualcuno) + di   *to tell (someone to do something)*

Il professore **ha detto agli studenti di** studiare bene per l'esame. Immagino che sia difficile!

The teacher told the students to study well for the exam. I imagine it will be difficult!

negare (a qualcuno) + di   *to deny/not allow (someone to do something)*

promettere (a qualucno) + di   *to promise (to do something for someone)*

ricordare (a qualcuno) + di   *to remind (someone to do something)*

vietare (a qualcuno) + di   *to prohibit someone from doing something*

Il mio capo **ci ha vietato di mangiare** mentre lavoriamo. Adesso dobbiamo andare alla mensa durante la pausa pranzo.

My boss prohibited us from eating while we work. Now we have to go to the cafeteria during our lunch break.

Appendix 4

The verbs in Appendix 4 require the preposition **con** + noun or the preposition **in** + noun/infinitive.

Learning Tip: There is no easy way to learn these verb/ preposition combinations. We suggest purchasing some index cards and a marker/pen, and writing the Italian verb and preposition on one side and the English equivalent on the other!

Verbs with the preposition **con:**

arrabbiarsi + con   *to be angry at*

avercela + con   *to have it up to here (with)*

combattere + con   *to fight against*

incavolarsi + con   *to get mad at*

litigare + con   *to argue with*

sposarsi + con   *to marry*

Marco **si è sposato con** Martina due anni fa a Como.

Marco married Martina two years ago in Como.

Verbs with the preposition **in:**

confidare + in   *to confide in*

laurearsi + in   *to get a degree in*

Mi sono laureato in scienze politiche quando vivevo a Roma.

I got a degree in political science when I was living in Rome.

sperare + in   *to hope for*

Appendix 5

The verbs in appendix 5 require the preposition **su** + noun.

Learning Tip: There is no easy way to learn these verb/preposition combinations. We suggest purchasing some index cards and a marker/pen, and writing the Italian verb and preposition on one side and the English equivalent on the other!

contare + su		*to count on*
insistere + su		*to insist on*

Se vuoi uscire con Marco, devo **insistere sul** coprifuoco! Devi tornare a casa prima di mezzanotte.

If you want to go out with Marco, I have to insist on a curfew! You have to be home before midnight.

puntare + su   *to bet on*

Mio padre è rimasto male quando ha saputo che **puntavo sulle** partite di basket.

My dad was upset when he found out I was betting on basketball games.

riflettere + su   *to reflect on*

salire + su   *to get up on*

scherzare + su   *to joke about*

Appendix 6

The adjectives and nouns in Appendix 6 require the preposition **a** + noun or infinitive.

Learning Tip: There is no easy way to learn these verb/ preposition combinations. We suggest purchasing some index cards and a marker/pen, and writing the Italian verb and preposition on one side and the English equivalent on the other!

adatto + a	*adapted for, suitable for*
addetto + a	*assigned to*
affezionato + a	*fond of*
allergico + a	*allergic to*
caro + a	*dear to*
contrario + a	*contrary to*
costretto + a	*forced to*
il **diritto** + a	*the right to*

Quando Tommaso è stato licenziato, gli ho detto che aveva **il diritto ad** una spiegazione dal suo capo.

When Tommaso was fired, I told him he had the right to an explanation from his boss.

occupato + a + *inf.*   *busy + doing something*

Senti, non rompermi! Sono **occupato a leggere** un libro impegnativo. Ci vuole molta concentrazione. Vai a trovare qualcosa da fare!

Listen, don't bother me! I'm busy reading a demanding book. It takes a lot of concentration. Go find something to do!

sconosciuto + a   *unknown to*

sensibile + a   *sensitive to*

utile + a   *useful for*

Questa guida è **utile agli** studenti di italiano perché aiuta a spiegare le regole e gli usi delle preposizioni.

This guide is useful for students studying Italian because it helps to explain the rules and uses of prepositions.

Appendix 7

The adjectives and nouns in Appendix 7 require the preposition **di** + noun.

Learning Tip: There is no easy way to learn these verb/preposition combinations. We suggest purchasing some index cards and a marker/pen, and writing the Italian verb and preposition on one side and the English equivalent on the other!

ansioso + di	*anxious to*
carico + di	*loaded with*
certo + di	*certain of*
colpevole + di	*guilty of*
contento + di	*happy with*

Sono **contenta di** voi! Avete sistemato la stanza e avete pulito i piatti. Grazie mille!

I am happy with you! You cleaned your room and washed the dishes. Thank you very much!

coperto + di	*covered with*
fornito + di	*furnished with*
la **mancanza** + di	*a lack of*
maniaco + di	*obsessed with*
l'**opportunità** + di	*an opportunity to*
pieno + di	*full of*
privo + di	*free of* (as in: *lacking in*)

Mia madre mangia solo il cibo bio perché è **privo di** sostanze chimiche e conservanti.*

*My mother eats only organic food because it is free of chemicals and preservatives.**

ricco + di	*rich in*
sorpreso + di	*surprised at*
stufo + di	*fed up with*

*Remember that the noun **il preservativo** does not mean *preservatives* but *condom*. The word for *preservatives* is **i conservanti**.

Appendix 8

In Appendix 1-5, we saw how some prepositions are paired with certain verbs. The same can be said of nouns and adjectives. Those profiled here are used with the prepositions **da** and **in**.

Learning Tip: There is no easy way to learn these verb/preposition combinations. We suggest purchasing some index cards and a marker/pen, and writing the Italian verb and preposition on one side and the English equivalent on the other!

Adjectives with the preposition **da**:

differente + da	*different from*
distante + da	*distant from*
diverso + da	*different from*
libero + da	*free from*
separato + da	*separated from*

Mario lavora in Inghilterra ma sua moglie è rimasta in Italia. È spesso triste perché è separato **dalla sua famiglia** e gli mancano i bambini.

Mario works in England, but his wife remained in Italy. He is often sad because he is separated from his family and misses his children.

Adjectives with the preposition **in**:

abile + in	*adept at*
bravo + in	*good at*
il **dottorato** + in	*a doctorate in*

Mio fratello ha il **dottorato in** inglese; ha studiato in Canada.

My brother has a doctorate in English; he studied in Canada.

esperto + in	*expert in*
lento + in	*slow to*

Non chiedere mai a Franco che vuoi una mano. È **lento nel*** rispondere e quando risponde alla fine è sempre troppo tardi.

Don't ever ask Franco that you want a hand. He is slow to respond and when he does respond, he is always too late.

*****NB**: When using **in** with infinitives, the in must become **nel**. Remember that infinitives, when used as nouns, are masculine!

This page intentionally left blank -- use it to take notes as you study!

This page intentionally left blank -- use it to take notes as you study!

This page intentionally left blank -- use it to take notes as you study!

This page intentionally left blank -- use it to take notes as you study!